Peace Harmony

Haiku Poetry

Dragica Ohashi

Indicates the color
of the new era Reiwa
plum flower

At sunset
a bouquet of peony
in the cloud

Forest in new dress
as a fairy tale princess
cherry magic wand

Drop of summer rain
write message on bamboo tree
Tanabata Day

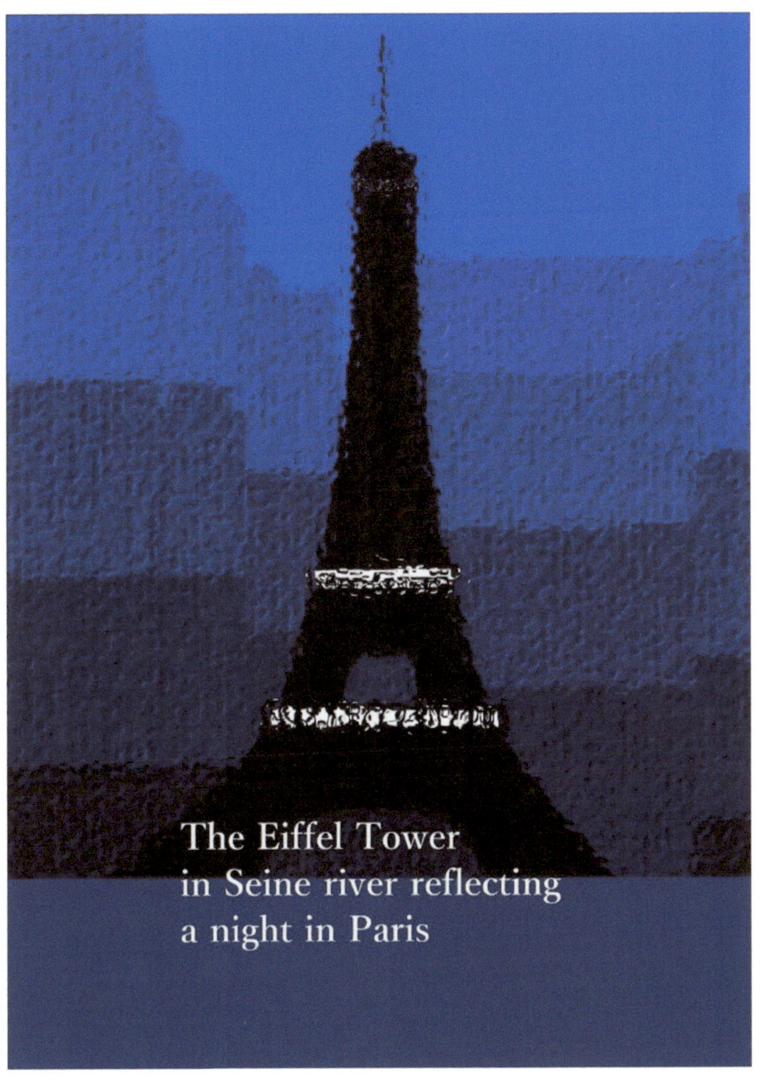
The Eiffel Tower
in Seine river reflecting
a night in Paris

Pink canvas
reminiscent of cherry tree
river creation

On the tender leaf
a cloud of inspiration
poet writing tips

Poetry night
the meadow of stars
spreading verses

Particles of bread
bitter and sweet taste today
waiting for cherry

Blue Moon ~
softness of night sky
come down to Earth

l catch the star spark
the blue sky over the lake
reflecting poem

Autumn verses
they sing like raindrops
in color of tears

An invisible thread
linking people to nature
gold leaf

Pen of lilac
whispering song of the valley
sweet flower home

Last leaf down
after pruning a tree
before autumn falls

Willow branches
bent toward the ground
hide the tears

Wild rose
the song of cicada
for her ~

Olive fruit
growing under the sun
ocean blue

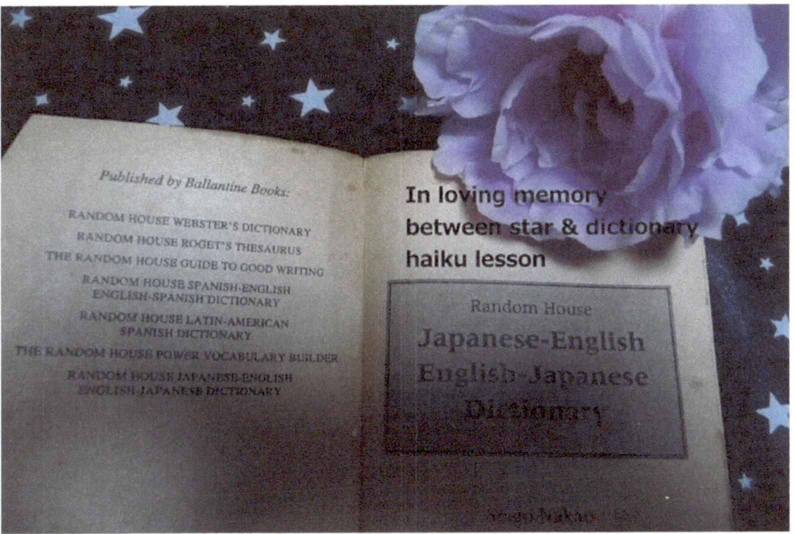
Published by Ballantine Books:

RANDOM HOUSE WEBSTER'S DICTIONARY
RANDOM HOUSE ROGET'S THESAURUS
THE RANDOM HOUSE GUIDE TO GOOD WRITING
RANDOM HOUSE SPANISH-ENGLISH
ENGLISH-SPANISH DICTIONARY
RANDOM HOUSE LATIN-AMERICAN
SPANISH DICTIONARY
THE RANDOM HOUSE POWER VOCABULARY BUILDER
RANDOM HOUSE JAPANESE-ENGLISH
ENGLISH-JAPANESE DICTIONARY

In loving memory
between star & dictionary
haiku lesson

Random House
Japanese-English
English-Japanese
Dictionary

Sandy beach
in the cloudy afternoon
a silvery sea

Sunset
over the castle
a sparkle

FANTASY COSMOS
LOOKING TO THE SKY
SEASON OF FALL

Summer Rose
just like a pearl from sea
bloom on my book

Colorless wind
touch of the brush painting
sumi-e ink

Glowing tulips
in the dark night
far away

Beach sand
footprints invisible
under the wave

Lullaby ~
a story for good sleep
moon light

old stone bridge
over the mountain river
olive & makia grow

Blue sky
a tapestry of clouds
endless

High in the sky
over the mountain and lake
puffy lavender clouds

Casablanca lily
forever last on picture
summer memory

Song of sorrow
cicada stopping to sing
on fig leaf

Iris flower
stand for hope
in forest

Haiku princess
twikling in the sky
new bright star

Fresh paint
digital meadow scenery
on the computer

Skeleton leaf
in my art book
from spring

Yoro Falls
in the deep forest on mountain
season of fresh green